THE 12 TOP ESTATE PLANNING TOOLS

THE 12 TOP
ESTATE PLANNING TOOLS

A NEWLY UPDATED GUIDE TO ESTATE TAX SAVING STRATEGIES

Paul R Marriott

President

PO Box 3, Corvallis, OR 97339

541-757-9911 or 800-724-8224

paul@marriottorganization.com

ISBN-13: 9781508482079
ISBN-10: 1508482071
Library of Congress Control Number: 2015915895
CreateSpace Independent Publishing Platform
North Charleston, South Carolina

FOREWORD

Procrastination. It's a word we might hate to hear, especially when we are talking about ourselves. The heavies in the field of psychology tell us that underlying fears are associated with the object of procrastination, and that is why we opt to do something else. In my own case, I like to think that it's simply a matter of preferring to do something else, or that an at-the-moment item is more important. Sadly for most folks (yours truly included), estate planning is an area in which many of us procrastinate.

After forty-plus years in the financial-services business, I have heard some amazing reasons for postponing estate planning. Some are humorous, some sad, but the bottom line is that estate planning often gets postponed until a situation of imminent demise occurs. You are lucky if you leave the planet slowly, because it affords you some time to put a plan together. Some are not so lucky. Cobbled together in a hurry, any estate plan is still better than no plan, but in the planning business, *sooner* is valued exponentially more than *later*.

In working with clients over the years, it seems to me that one of the main reasons for procrastinating on an estate plan is unfamiliarity with the entire process. Confusion can reign when you start down the planning road, and often that confusion can bring the planning process to a screeching halt. There is no lack of information on estate planning. The web is full of it, and so are folks at that cocktail party or coffee break. What seems to confuse people is how all of the different planning strategies work and how they might apply to a given individual's circumstances. I often hear comments like, "I can't figure out the language in this document" and "How does this work?" Or worse: "What are you talking about?"

A better understanding of how various tools used in the estate-planning process work can clear the fog that often derails a would-be planner. It is with this thought in mind that I launched into the idea of writing an article in 2003 titled "Common Estate-Planning Tools." I designed it to give both planners and potential planners a brief synopsis of what each tool was and how it worked.

As I write this new version early in September 2015, and with a different title, our Congress has finally spoken on estate, gift, and generation-skipping taxes. In 2011, we got new rules regarding these taxes, which have been reunified, modified, and indexed. As a result, some tremendous opportunities were presented. I will allude to these within the framework of this booklet, but if there ever was a time for reviewing your estate plan, it is now.

And so, with the hope of giving you a snapshot of the tools that, in my opinion, are the "Top Twelve" (in keeping with my noncompete agreement with David Letterman), and with even higher hopes of moving you away from procrastination and providing you with a small jolt of energy, I give you the 2015 updated version, titled "The Top Twelve Estate-Planning Tools."

It is my fondest hope that if you need planning (and even the smallest estates do), you will have that first discussion with your estate-planning lawyer, accountant, or financial professional. Additionally, if you would like a longer explanation of a particular tool discussed here, just give us a call or drop us an e-mail. You will never see how your plan will ultimately work out, but it well could be one of the more important things you ever do.

Paul R. Marriott, CLU, ChFC, CAIA
September 2015

CHAPTER 1

THE WILL

I n any list of estate-planning tools, a will should come first. It is the cornerstone of anyone's postmortem plan, and it is the most comprehensive document available to an estate owner to see that his or her wishes are carried out. We will discuss a living trust (an *inter vivos* trust) and its advantages, but even if you have a living trust, you generally need to complete a will, even if your estate is small.

Why You Need a Will

So why do you need a will? Most people realize that a will enables them to designate beneficiaries of their estate. There can be very broad designations, as well as extremely narrow designations, down to specific pieces of property. But all of these types of designations fall into the category of dispositive provisions of the will (i.e., who gets what).

Your will also identifies members of your family. This seems almost unnecessary except that a will can often include language that transfers property equally to "my children." Clearing up who those children are is important. In younger families, the will also usually identifies who a guardian will be for minor children in the event of both estate owners' deaths.

Equally important to the act of identifying your children is identifying your spouse, if you have one. It's amazing to me how many times we look at wills and find bequests to people who are no longer in the picture—especially former spouses. If you're getting the idea that a will needs to be reviewed periodically, you have grasped my most enduring plea of this entire piece.

The Will's Important Role in Tax Planning

The will can provide for many benefits at your death. In addition to stating what property goes to which heirs, it identifies the all-important person who will be your executor or personal representative. Most important for an estate of any size, however, is the opportunity to facilitate some tax planning. Since 1981, the government has allowed a full marital deduction for property passing between spouses, either at death or via a gift during a lifetime. That means no taxes. The problem here is that too many unreviewed wills still simply leave the balance of an estate to the surviving spouse, and most of the time, the spouse's will reads the same way. So what's the problem? Well, that's one of the big stories these days in the estate-planning business.

The problem used to be that any estate-tax credit did not get used by the first spouse to die when all property was simply willed to the surviving spouse. Because the credit is applied to each decedent's estate, a spouse dying first who left all property to the surviving spouse would not pay tax, but only by virtue of the full marital deduction. When the second spouse died, only one credit would be available. Congress actually fixed this problem in 2011 when it allowed any unused credit from the first spouse's death to be carried over to the second estate. For 2015, the credit allowed provides an exempt amount from federal estate taxation of $5.43 million for each estate. This means that a couple would have an exempt amount from federal estate taxation of $10.86 million. Great, but...

The "but" here concerns a specific state's actions with regard to estate and inheritance taxes. Most states used to use what they called a "pickup tax" for their own collection process from people dying and owing federal estate tax. The federal estate-tax-return form, Form 706, allows a credit against the federal tax for state death taxes paid. In the past, most states mandated that whatever that credit was would be their tax. Simple. Oregon, Washington, and most other states using this taxable amount simply called it a "pickup tax" because they simply picked up the credit as their tax. As the federal government began to increase the exempt amount, however, most states began to realize decreasing revenues from this source of taxation were either here or right around the corner, and they enacted their own new estate and inheritance transfer rules and tax rates.

Every state has a somewhat different taxation idea. Oregon would probably be fairly illustrative of new state rates, with an exempt amount of $1 million per person. On the very next dollar, the tax rate is 10 percent, and it moves to the top rate of 16 percent on any amount in excess of $9.5 million. The bigger problem here for nearly all state estate and inheritance taxes is that there is no carryover for any unused credit. So, jumping back to the will, you may want to think seriously about how you plan to use both exempt amounts at the state level, even though it is no longer a problem for federal estate-tax filings. Check out all of this with your favorite estate-planning attorney. It could save your estate many thousands of dollars.

So a properly drawn will takes into account the effect of estate taxes at the state level, as well as the federal level, and uses language and testamentary trusts (trusts created at death) to take advantage of the exempt amounts available in both estates. I'll save the mechanics of one way this is accomplished for a later piece, but the starting point is your will.

————

I haven't touched on many other aspects and wonders of the will, but I'm hoping you already have grasped the importance of this document. Even if you have a will that you think "does the job," take it out once a year (I like the end-of-the-year holidays, although that may be too late for year-end planning) and read it. If it does what you want it to do, great. If it doesn't or, more commonly, if something is unclear, then give your lawyer a call and have that friendly chat with him or her about your findings. You might be very happy that you did.

I can't overstress the importance of this annual review. Congress and each individual state are constantly changing the way things work at death, specifically the way estate taxes are imposed and to what extent. As I've noted above, since 2001, most states have changed how they tax an estate, so reviewing your will with these new state inheritance taxes in mind can definitely be beneficial. Try the web for your particular state's estate or inheritance tax form that your estate might be required to file. You can learn a lot from that form and at least put together questions for your advisors.

In addition to all of the above, don't forget your opportunity to create other trusts at your death. The potential list is long here, depending on what you want to do. Your lawyer can talk to you about the pros and cons of skipping a generation with a bequest, setting up educational trusts for children and grandchildren, stretching out IRAs to heirs, and many other useful tools initiated inside your will. Also, don't forget to think about charitable bequests, which can help your estate-tax picture and provide a tremendous boost to a charity you have been involved with.

The will is the start to any intelligent estate plan, and for busy people, it is the easiest thing to put off until later. "Later" sometimes arrives unexpectedly, however, and often with unintended results. Lawyers draft wills. Even those who don't specialize in estate planning can either prepare a simple will (if that is what is required) or transfer you to a partner or other firm where a more comprehensive job can be done, if necessary. Without a will, a decedent's estate is distributed by a court-appointed administrator. Almost worse is the old and outdated will that bears no resemblance to a decedent's current wishes. Read your will before your family has to. You may find it interesting.

CHAPTER 2

THE LIVING TRUST

A living trust may be your second most valuable estate-planning document. It is exactly what is says it is: a trust created and maintained during your lifetime. Planners also call these trusts *inter vivos* trusts.

Benefits of a Trust

The beauty of this trust is that it allows all assets that are part of the trust to be transferred to the trust beneficiaries without hitting probate. Probate deals with anything that passes solely by your will. That means that any property passing via a beneficiary designation or through any fashion other than a will (such as joint tenancy) will automatically escape the probate process. That means savings to the estate because probate fees can be sizable. It also means there would most definitely be an easy transfer because most living trust documents name successor trustees, as well as beneficiaries who take over in the event of the death or resignation of the trustor (the person putting the trust together).

You Are the Trustee

So who is the trustee of this nice trust? You are. Yes, in most cases, you are the trustee of your own trust. That way, you have complete control over the assets in the trust and can make changes to the trust language as you see fit. As mentioned above, you would generally name a successor trustee or trustees, and quite often, the successors are also the beneficiaries. So why do it in the first place? Because all assets in the trust escape probate, and the transfer of assets is extremely easy.

Normally, a lawyer drafting a living trust for a client will include some additional documents that can be helpful to family members. These can include a durable power of attorney, a HIPAA privacy statement for hospitals and doctors you and your family might need information from, and a health directive. This directive expresses your preference regarding the use of life-sustaining hospital equipment.

Two Interesting Facts

Here are two other interesting facts about the living trust:

1. It does nothing to exempt you from estate taxes.
2. You can resign from being trustee and allow your successor trustees to take over. This may make sense in your later life or if you are battling an extended illness. You simply put together (via your lawyer) a letter that documents your resignation, and your successors take over. It's really that easy.

Because you have complete control over the assets, all trust property will be included in your gross estate at your death.

So escape probate, yes; escape estate taxes, no.

All in all, a living trust is an excellent tool for making smooth transfers of property without much hassle and with complete privacy. Probated property is always listed for public record, but trust property is not. The privacy issue alone may well be worth using this tool. And yes, I do think spouses should each have their own living trust, even though they are naming each other as a beneficiary. It is extremely useful to have the trust in effect when the first spouse dies.

Ask your planner about a living trust if you don't have one already. There are a number of virtues to this nice tool. It is a far better way to hold assets than in some joint-tenancy arrangement. The discussion you have with a planner about this tool can be an eye opener that leads to completing an estate plan.

CHAPTER 3

ANNUAL GIFTING

Annual gifting has been around for years, and it can be an important yet simple estate-planning tool. However, it often gets overlooked. Currently an individual can give away $14,000 annually per recipient. That means that if you have four children, for example, you can give away $56,000 per year ($14,000 per child) each year. But it gets better. Your spouse can join the giving and double the results. In the situation above, that amounts to $112,000 of tax-free gifts per year.

Some folks are reluctant to make gifts to children. The old saying regarding giving to children is a good one: "If you want to see how your kids will spend your money after you're gone, give them some now, and see what they do with it." This may or may not be a good strategy, but annual gifts can be an important part of an estate plan, especially when you are trying to implement a business succession plan. In this case, the form of the business interest is extremely important. I discuss this a bit in the description of another tool, the family LLC.

Two Tips for Annual Giving

Annual giving often involves making gifts of life insurance premiums to an irrevocable trust to provide a substantial source of tax-free liquidity with which estate taxes and settlement costs can be paid. Substantial securities portfolios are excellent candidates for annual gifting sources as well. There are two important things to remember here:

1. Don't squander this tool. Think seriously about how it can be a part of your overall plan and how it should be implemented.
2. The annual gift will pass tax-free to the people receiving the gift, but their basis in the property that they receive will be the same as yours. That could trigger a larger capital-gains tax when the asset is sold. Most annual gifts are cash, so this issue doesn't normally come into play until the gifts get quite large, as is the case with lifetime gifts covered in the next section. Cash and fast-growing assets are generally the best candidates for annual gifts, but listed securities and fractional ownership in a family-owned business could work well too.

All in all, annual gifting can achieve some amazing results over a period of time, and it can be implemented as easily as writing a check.

CHAPTER 4

LIFETIME GIFTING

A s nice as annual giving is, lifetime giving is even better, and the new changes to the law that I mentioned in the foreword give us a tremendous opportunity. I mentioned that we now have a reunified gift and estate tax. Even though the exempt amount for estates began moving up in 2001, the lifetime-gift exemption stayed at $1 million per donor. Not until 2011 did the lifetime-gift exemption become the same as the estate-tax exemption once again.

Tax Savings and Other Benefits

With the lifetime exclusion amount in 2015 for a gift at the same exempt amount as for estate taxes (i.e., $5.43 million per person or $10.86 million per couple), some extensive transfers can be made without tax. Wow! No matter how sizable your estate may be, this exclusion is a big one. And with discounts available for minority interest and lack of marketability, you can make a substantial gift to transfer important assets to the next generation.

Interestingly, the generation-skipping exemption is also currently at the $5.43 million level as well. Although this is definitely an area that needs the fine touch of your estate-planning attorney, you can realize huge leverage and estate savings for several generations by skipping a generation with some gifts. This strategy and nearly all of the others I mention are definitely not "do-it-yourself" jobs, but a competent tax lawyer can be a tremendous investment for you and your family. Scout around and check referrals, and as strange as it might seem to some folks, the tax lawyer can actually be your friend—especially in the area of generation-skipping and lifetime giving.

Business transition and succession plans fit nicely here. Likewise, here's a chance for an estate owner to distribute assets equitably while attempting to "even up" ownership of assets among heirs that are either inside or outside of the family business. Also, this could be your opportunity to make a sizable one-time "gift" into life insurance owned by an irrevocable trust and get that contract to a paid-up status. If you use your imagination, you will probably do far better than I have in coming up with excellent ways to use this quite powerful tool.

Get Your Lawyer's Help

And once more, a caveat: be sure to contact your planning lawyer here. You will need to file a gift-tax return (Form 709) and let the IRS know what you are doing in that return. Some clients don't like inviting those good-humor folks into the picture, but your lawyer should tell you the advantages of doing so. There are a number of advantages of filing the return, not the least of which is starting the clock running on the statute of limitations for improperly valuing the gift. Absent the return, the valuation issue can stay open until your death and would be settled only after an estate audit.

If you have been itching to make some transfers but the amount has been too big, *now* may be your time.

CHAPTER 5

SURVIVORSHIP LIFE INSURANCE

To my knowledge, only two companies were writing survivorship life insurance prior to 1981. In that year, the Economic Recovery Tax Act was passed. A full marital deduction for estate-tax purposes was included in that bill. Before that, you could leave everything to a surviving spouse, but only half of it would be eligible for the marital deduction. As a result, taxes would be due at first death if the taxable estate was large enough.

Following the 1981 Tax Act, it didn't take much imagination to determine that the opportune time for most estates to pay any tax due was at the death of the second spouse of a married couple, because no tax would be due unless you wanted to pay those taxes at the death of the first spouse. In all my years in this business, I have yet to see any case in which paying taxes at the first death was the desire of the estate owner.

With most estate taxes due at the second death, the survivorship or second-to-die life insurance contract began to blossom. Within a year, nearly every major company that we dealt with had a survivorship policy available.

Advantages over Single-Life Contracts

Survivorship life insurance has some terrific advantages over single-life contracts for estate purposes:

1. The proceeds come in exactly when your executor would need them to pay estate taxes, state inheritance taxes, administrative costs, and anything else that would rear its ugly head following the death of the second spouse.
2. Survivorship coverage is normally a bit less expensive because the mortality cost embedded in the policy is stretched over the two lives rather than just one.
3. If one spouse might have insurability problems due to health issues, the healthy spouse can balance out that underwriting condition, and coverage can be implemented at a very competitive rate.

Reasons to Use Life Insurance to Pay Estate Costs
So why use any life insurance to pay estate costs, anyway?

1. The primary reason is that the proceeds are *free* of estate, gift, generation-skipping, and income taxes. I should add the words "when arranged properly." And that, of course, is your lawyer's job.
2. Also, there is a tremendous discount when figuring your payment (premium) over the years to a normal mortality and comparing it to digging the liquidity out of the estate within nine months of death.
3. And of course there is the certainty that liquid cash will be available for estate settlement costs rather than having the executor borrow or sell assets that could be of value in the hands of heirs.

Arranging this coverage properly to escape estate taxation involves third-party ownership. Now and then, children are made owners of this type of insurance coverage. But normally, the preferred vehicle for ownership is the irrevocable trust, which is discussed next. In all of the cases I have written over the years involving survivorship life insurance, only two were written for nonestate purposes. For settling estates, it is a tremendous tool. It's the only one of the entire dozen that brings in cash— a much-desired commodity when dealing with settlement costs.

CHAPTER 6

IRREVOCABLE TRUST OR IRREVOCABLE LIFE INSURANCE TRUST (ILIT)

I mentioned the irrevocable trust in the preceding section, but let's take a closer look, beginning with a definition of this fine tool. Its primary use in the estate plan is to be the owner and beneficiary of life insurance that is to be used for settling estate-related costs at death. And it is irrevocable!

The Pros and Cons of Irrevocability

The fact that this trust cannot be revoked has advantages and disadvantages. The primary advantage is that once this trust is formed, the trustor (the person who makes the trust) cannot withdraw assets from the trust. This is an advantage because the loss of power over this trust means that all proceeds in the trust at death would generally not be part of the decedent's estate.

The disadvantage is that you may change your mind at some point regarding beneficiaries and other aspects of the trust, and with only small exceptions, the trust cannot be changed. I once asked an estate-planning attorney if he knew of any way to get rid of an irrevocable trust. He replied, "Only one: rip it up."

A New Wrinkle

There has been a new wrinkle in the past few years on "decanting" an irrevocable trust. The folks that put that name on this procedure must have been drinking wine at the time as it works just like decanting an old Mouton Rothschild Bordeaux into a new glass decanter for serving. It involves forming a new irrevocable trust and moving the assets, beneficiaries, and most provisions to the new trust. You might be more interested in the Bordeaux, but the pouring process is about the same—wine in one case and legal provisions in the other. Not all states allow decanting, and, as you might guess, the rules don't allow for much leeway in changes from the old trust. Nevertheless, this can be a tremendous opportunity when changes might be sorely needed to an old irrevocable trust. Once again, a *good* tax lawyer (could there possibly be bad ones?) will be your friend here, especially one who has experience in this area.

In using an irrevocable trust to own life insurance, all proceeds (again, income-tax-free) at death fall outside of the estate. Yet the language of the trust makes it possible for the trustee to use the proceeds to either buy estate assets or loan money to the estate to pay taxes and other estate expenses.

About Premium Payments

Here is a word of advice about premium payments for the insurance: the payment has to be a gift to the trust. That gift needs some special handling, too, to qualify for the annual gift exclusion of $14,000. Any gift that does qualify for the annual exclusion needs to be a gift of "present interest." Generally, a gift to a trust is a gift of "future interest." Back in the late 1960s, a smart lawyer in the San Francisco Bay Area figured out how to turn an irrevocable trust gift into a gift of "present interest." He had the donors make the gift of an annual premium to the trust, and then he allowed the beneficiaries to withdraw that premium amount if they wanted it. If they did not want it, the gift-withdrawal power lapsed, and the money became part of the trust. This lawyer's client was named Mrs. Crummey (yes, I'm spelling it correctly), and today, irrevocable trusts with this provision are called Crummey trusts.

Each year when a premium is paid on life insurance held in an irrevocable trust, the gift of the premium is made to the trust, and the trustees notify the beneficiaries that they have the right to withdraw that gift during what is usually a thirty-day period. Once that period has elapsed, the trustee forwards the funds to the insurance carrier.

The irrevocable trust can be used for other purposes besides simply owning estate-earmarked life insurance, but far and away its most popular use is for this purpose. The number of annual gift exclusions that can be used is based on the number of beneficiaries. So with four children as beneficiaries, the annual gift you could make without taxation is $56,000 (4 × $14,000) or, with the spouse also giving, $112,000 per year. Where large amounts of life insurance are involved in an estate plan, this tool is almost always called for.

CHAPTER 7

FAMILY LIMITED LIABILITY COMPANY (LLC) OR FAMILY LIMITED PARTNERSHIP (FLP)

T he family limited liability company (LLC) or family limited partnership (FLP) is a tool that can have multiple uses in any estate plan. Probably its most popular use is facilitating gifts to another generation. It can be extremely effective in that capacity.

One desire of many estate planners is to transfer ownership for their clients without transferring much or any control. How can that be done? Enter the family LLC. The LLC is often formed by issuing one hundred different member interests, similar to forming a corporation and issuing shares of stock. All interests are of equal value, except that two interests carry the management rights to the LLC.

I know one lawyer who actually gets out a bag of one hundred poker chips to demonstrate how the family LLC works. All of the poker chips are white except for two red ones. The red chips carry the management rights (i.e., "control"), but they are not valued any more than the white ones. One red chip goes to Mr. Estate Owner, and the other goes to Mrs. Estate Owner.

They then begin giving away the "white chip" interests through a well-designed gifting plan. For business owners who would generally have additional problems giving away stock in a corporation or other forms of business interest, the family LLC is a package that can be very useful.

IRS Discounts

And did I mention the discounting of the gifts? Generally, the IRS allows two discounts for certain gifts of an entity: a discount for a minority interest (less than 50 percent) and a discount for lack of marketability. Your lawyer can best guide you on this. It is almost certain that an appraisal will need to be made of the entity in question, but the discounts are there. The minority interest discount has been a point of interest for the IRS in recent years in cases where one family owns all of the interests. But, certainly, the lack of marketability is still there and can be leveraged.

In addition to being a useful planning tool, most estate owners find that the family LLC is a dandy way to begin bringing the next generation into the business (those who might be coming in). Using an annual meeting to discuss the business of the LLC has proven to be an excellent planning session for all family members with LLC interests.

CHAPTER 8

_____

GRANTOR RETAINED ANNUITY TRUST (GRAT)

T
he grantor retained annuity trust (GRAT) is the first of the split-interest vehicles discussed in this booklet. It can be a lifesaver where a large asset needs to be transferred to another generation.
It works like this: A grantor (donor) places property into a GRAT, and the GRAT is set up to pay an income back to the grantor for a specific period and at a specific interest rate. At the end of the income period, the property is distributed to the beneficiaries of the trust. Normally, the grantor is the estate owner, and the beneficiaries are his or her children.

The Main Advantage of a GRAT

So why use a GRAT? The beauty of the GRAT is that you can drastically shrink the taxable value of a gift. Yes, gift taxes may be involved, but the rules governing GRATs allow you to subtract the present value of the income stream that would be retained from the value of the property in the GRAT when determining the actual value of the gift to be reported.

As you might guess, with the correct setting of the income and the discount rate, the present value could nearly be the same as the value of the property gifted to the GRAT in the first place. And this, of course, is the reason for using the GRAT. We have seen multimillion-dollar properties transferred to a GRAT with multimillion-dollar present-value income streams subtracted from those transfers, leaving the value of the gift for tax purposes well below the $100,000 mark. This easily fits into a grantor's annual gift-tax exclusion. It can be a dandy tool.

A Couple of Caveats

A couple of caveats are worth mentioning here:

1. Should you die during the income period of the GRAT, all property in the GRAT reverts back into your estate. Obviously, there is more leverage in a ten-year GRAT than a two-year GRAT, but the chances of dying before the end of the income period are increased.

2. Also, in the newest tax legislation that brought us all of the changes to the estate and gift taxes, GRATs were discussed. There was talk regarding new arrangements whereby extending a GRAT past two years will be forbidden. That threat has come and gone, but last year, President Obama had some fairly strong critical comments on GRATs in his 2015 budget discussion. So far, so good, as GRATs continue to be used quite successfully.

GRATs work best when you are attempting to transfer existing assets to the next generation with minimal tax impact. Assets that are likely to increase in value quickly are generally excellent candidates for use in a GRAT situation. In calculating the present value of the income stream to the donor, the rate used is the government's 7520 rate. The 7520 rate refers to the code section. Generally, the lower the rate, the better the leverage in transferring assets to the GRAT beneficiaries. The current 7520 rate is 2.2 percent for the month of September 2015. I consider GRATs a very viable tool in situations where they fit.

The GRAT's Cousin, the Qualified Personal Residence Trust (QPRT)

An interesting second cousin to the GRAT is an arrangement called the qualified personal residence trust (QPRT). This tool is used for transferring a primary residence or vacation residence to another generation. It essentially works in the same fashion as the GRAT mechanics mentioned above; you can shrink the taxable value of the gift substantially. There are some interesting ramifications to these types of trust arrangements. One is that you may be paying rent to your kids to live in your home. The QPRT is a dandy tool, however, for that second home that you want to stay in the family. Its ability to shrink the gift makes it a very desirable tool.

CHAPTER 9

CHARITABLE REMAINDER TRUST (CRT)

The second "split-interest" vehicle we will look at is the charitable remainder trust (CRT). This trust allows a grantor to donate property to a trust and, once again, take back an income—generally for life. At the end of the grantor's life, the property will be passed on to a charity or charities named in the trust.

Because a charity is involved, an immediate charitable deduction is available for the year in which the trust is formed. The amount of that deduction is calculated similarly to the GRAT gift calculation above—the present value of the income stream is subtracted from the value of the property transferred to the trust. Because most CRTs pay the income over a lifetime, life expectancy is the number used for calculating the number of years in this scenario.

A CRT's Main Advantage

The big advantage of a CRT is that property is immediately transferred to a charity when the charity is the trustee, and the charity will usually sell the property to create funds it will use to pay an income to the grantor. At the time of that sale, no capital gain is recognized by the grantor, and of course, the charity is exempt. The grantor will pay taxes on the income in an interesting fashion. If there was gain, his or her income may be taxed at capital-gains rates. If any income is generated by the charity, the grantor's income could be taxed at ordinary income rates, and if the income is normally exempt, as in the case of municipal bonds, the grantor's income is likewise exempt. The accounting for the trust income is far beyond the scope of this booklet, but if you have an interest in how this all works, give us a call. Some years back, my wife and I set up our own CRT, so I am intimately acquainted with them.

The Ideal CRT Candidate

The ideal candidate for a CRT is a charitable individual with a high-value, low-basis asset who would like to turn that asset into an income stream for retirement. A sale would obviously trigger capital-gains taxes, but if the property were placed in a CRT, the charity could use the entire asset to generate the income for the grantor.

Often, "wealth replacement" life insurance is purchased with a portion of the income from the CRT. This arrangement is entered into to avoid depriving the family heirs of the value of the asset transferred to the CRT. In a lot of cases, the insurance coverage can be paid for out of the CRT income. The result is that the grantor still ends up with more money than he or she would have by selling the asset and taking an after-tax income stream from those sale proceeds.

For the high-value, low-basis asset owner who wants to turn on the income stream, this tool can work wonders, *and* the property that is transferred is out of the grantor's estate.

CHAPTER 10

CHARITABLE LEAD TRUST

The charitable lead trust (CLT) is almost the mirror image of the charitable remainder trust (CRT) just described above. With the CRT, we put property into trust, received an income, and, at death, the property went to the charity. In contrast, with the charitable lead trust, we put property into trust, and the income is paid to the charity for a specific number of years. At the end of that period, the trust property is transferred to the trust beneficiaries, who normally are children or other family heirs.

Once again, a "split-interest" gift is involved. In this case, a gift is being made to the beneficiaries, who are ultimately receiving the trust property. As calculated earlier, the grantor is allowed to subtract the present value of the income stream that goes to charity from the transferred property in determining the value of the gift. In the same fashion as the GRAT calculation, we can adjust the income stream, interest rate, and time period to get a present-value number for the income stream that would be nearly what the property value was. This means that our gift would be extremely small and even manageable within the annual gift exclusion.

The Ideal CLT Candidate

An ideal candidate for using this excellent tool is someone with a large asset that probably generated an income (although this latter feature is not essential) and who wants to transfer it to another generation. It would be ideal for someone already making gifts to a charity because he or she can substitute those current gifts with gifts from the lead trust and have the tremendously discounted asset transferred to the heirs.

We don't see lead trusts all that often, but in the right case, they can be unbelievably effective. Certainly, if you have charitable intent now and are looking to move a large asset to a second generation, check this one out. Interests in a family LLC also may be an appropriate asset for a CLT.

CHAPTER 11

INSTALLMENT SALE TO A DEFECTIVE GRANTOR TRUST (IDIT)

This one gets just a tad complicated, but let's try to simplify it and figure out why I am considering it in my "top twelve" list. Once again, I am including this tool because of its ability to move a large asset out of an estate with little impact in terms of taxes.

The arrangement calls for creating a grantor trust first. To be a grantor trust, certain features must be present, and all lawyers putting these trusts together know how to do that. The grantor and the trust are deemed to be one and the same for income-tax purposes, and this is key.

The grantor then makes a "seed" gift to the trust (yes, it is a taxable gift), and the trustee of the trust then enters into an installment sale of a large asset from the grantor. There are many ways to generate enough income within the trust (including additional gifts from the grantor) to make the installment payments to the grantor for the asset. The instant the sale is put together, the property is out of the grantor's estate (for estate-tax purposes) because the IRS looks at this transaction as a typical sale of property, which it is. The interesting thing, however, is that no capital-gains tax is due on the sale because it is made to the grantor trust, which is deemed to be the same as the grantor (for income-tax purposes.) In other words, there is no tax for selling to yourself.

It is a completed transaction, however, for estate-tax purposes, and that is where the beauty of this arrangement lies. It is not a sale for income-tax purposes, but a completed sale for estate-tax purposes.

At the end of the installment period, the trust can generally fold up, with the property being distributed to the trust beneficiaries. There are some tax speed bumps to be aware of in this arrangement, but for the individual wanting to move a large asset like a family business, the IDIT can be a very dear friend.

CHAPTER 12

Dynasty Trust

A dynasty trust is an irrevocable trust that stretches over a number of generations. It can be set up either while the estate owner is alive or after death via a testamentary directive. Its purpose is to provide money to future generations for any number of reasons.

Most states have a rule against perpetuities, meaning that you can't stretch trusts out indefinitely. A few states have not enacted these laws against perpetuities, and they are the states in which nearly all dynasty-type trusts are cited. Two that we are familiar with are South Dakota and Alaska.

An irrevocable trust in those jurisdictions is funded with cash, other assets, or life insurance, and a trust is very specific about who can receive funds from the trust and for what purpose. Generally, these trusts are created for funding educational costs for future generations. We have also seen them used for highly unusual purposes, including ownership of such things as jewelry (like wedding rings) that may be worn by spouses of family members, but come divorce, those pieces are returned to the custody of the trust.

This tool can have a very long-lasting effect on the welfare of the family for generations to come. We don't see that many, but for the long-range planner, this tool can make a tremendous difference to future family members.

CONCLUSION

S o that's it. We've run through just some of the tools a planner can use to optimize his or her assets. New tools emerge all the time, such as one I saw recently called the Beneficiary Defective Income Trust (BDIT). The ones I have described are the ones that we see most of the time and have the most general usefulness.

I have touched on just the high points of each of these tools, but if you would like more information about any one of these in particular, I have reams of information, some of which might even be readable. It is entirely possible that by the time you read this, Congress will have made changes to the law that will change the viability of each tool I have discussed, so make sure you have that chat with your tax lawyer before diving in. Each tool has its own purpose, but as always, what is called for in most situations is an overall plan to meet your estate objectives.

Thanks for reading. I look forward to a very active balance for 2015 and on into 2016 in the estate-planning field as the possibilities of the recent changes begin to unfold. I wish you good health and happy prosperity.

www.ingramcontent.com/pod-product-compliance
Lightning Source LLC
Chambersburg PA
CBHW070751180526
45168CB00004B/1587